not a guide to

Kensington & Chelsea

Simon Webb

The History Press

First published 2012

The History Press
The Mill, Brimscombe Port
Stroud, Gloucestershire, GL5 2QG
www.thehistorypress.co.uk

British Library Cataloguing in Publication Data.
A catalogue record for this book is available from the British Library.

ISBN 978 0 7524 6633 0

Typesetting and origination by The History Press
Printed in Great Britain

Contents

Introduction

The Royal Borough of Kensington and Chelsea: healthy, wealthy and ... cramped.

Singapore and Hong Kong are reckoned to be two of the most densely populated territories on the planet, containing respectively 7,148 and 6,348 people per square kilometre. Surprisingly, the Royal Borough of Kensington and Chelsea is more than twice as crowded as either of these places, cramming an astounding 13,244 people into every one of its 12 square kilometres, according to the 2001 census. Fortunately, there are compensations for living in such a crowded place.

Residents of the borough have the highest life expectancy in the UK.

The Royal Borough of Kensington and Chelsea has a higher proportion of top earners, i.e. those on over £60,000 a year, than any other local authority district in the UK.

Perhaps as a direct consequence of all those high earners squeezing together in the second smallest borough in London, the five most expensive places to buy property in Britain are all in Kensington and Chelsea. The average price of a house in the W8 postal district is £1.75 million.

The general health of those living here is very good. This might be connected with the residents' enthusiasm for exercise; over a quarter of people living in Kensington and Chelsea take part in a sport or visit a swimming pool or gym three times a week.

The Royal Connection

Before we go any further, why is Kensington and Chelsea a royal borough?

It is one of only eight places in Britain allowed to prefix its name with 'Royal', the others being Berkshire, Windsor, Tunbridge Wells, Kingston upon Thames, Leamington Spa, Wootton Bassett and, from 2012, Greenwich.

Kensington has held this title since the death of Queen Victoria in 1901, and it was awarded in recognition of the fact that Victoria was born in the borough, in Kensington Palace. The Royal Borough of Kensington and Chelsea, or RBKC as it is often known, has many other connections with royalty. Over the page are a few kings and queens who have lived in RBKC.

THE QUEEN ON THE MORNING OF HER ACCESSION, JUNE 20, 1837.

Henry VIII moved to Chelsea for a time, after being impressed with the then village after visiting Thomas More there.

Anne of Cleves was Henry's fourth wife and lived in Chelsea after her divorce. She also died there.

Catherine Parr was Henry's last wife, and also lived in Chelsea.

Elizabeth I lived in Chelsea as a child.

William III set up home in Kensington Palace because he was asthmatic and wanted to escape the smoke of London. He died there.

Mary II was William III's wife and also lived and then died at Kensington Palace.

Queen Anne lived at Kensington Palace.

George I lived in Kensington Palace until his death.

George II was the last reigning monarch to live in Kensington.

Queen Victoria was born in Kensington Palace and grew up there.

That reigning monarchs have, since Victoria, had their official residence at Buckingham Palace rather than Kensington does not mean that members of royalty are no longer to be found at Kensington Palace: Prince Charles and Diana lived there from 1981 onwards, and Diana was still a resident up to her death in 1997. Princess Margaret lived here, and the two latest royals to make this palace their home are the Duke and Duchess of Cambridge, better known, of course, as Prince William and Kate Middleton.

Origins

RBKC has only existed in its present form since the reorganisation of London's boroughs in 1965; before that, it was two separate boroughs. Kensington and Chelsea's history, though, stretches back a good deal earlier than 1965! Kensington is first mentioned in the Domesday Book, compiled in 1086. It is referred to as Chenesitone, which is more or less a phonetic rendering of Kensignetun, Kenisgne's fields or meadows. The derivation of Chelsea's name is equally ancient: it is a corruption of the Anglo-Saxon *Cealc Hythe*, meaning 'Chalk Wharf or landing place'.

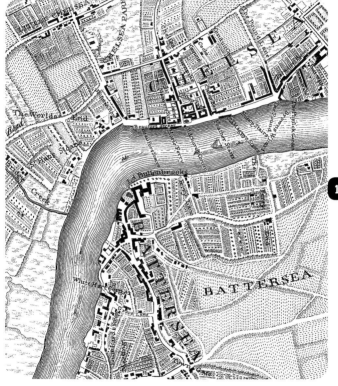

CHELSEA

CHELSEA PARK

The Worlds End
Road

Hall Shoar

Creek

Beaufort Street

Battersea

Whitewall

BATTERSEA

Kensington and Chelsea may today be the epitome of sophisticated urban living, but it was not always so. In the eighteenth century, Kensington and Chelsea were both villages a few miles outside London. The surrounding countryside was infested with highwaymen who preyed on those travelling to London. On Sunday evenings, a bell was rung in Kensington to assemble all those who wished to travel to London, so that they could form a large party to deter footpads and highwaymen. A similar arrangement was in place at Hyde Park, so that travellers to Kensington could also join together in groups. Charles Dickens refers to the dangers of travelling between London and those two villages to the west in his novel *Barnaby Rudge*: 'few would travel to Chelsea, unarmed and unattended'. In the 1730s, a witness at the Old Bailey testified that he had seen William Gordon, a notorious highwayman, mounted on his horse inside the kitchen of an inn near Knightsbridge, waiting for lone travellers whom he could rob.

ST. VOLODYMYR

RULER OF UKRAINE
980 – 1015

ERECTED BY UKRAINIANS IN GREAT BRITAIN IN
1988
TO CELEBRATE THE ESTABLISHMENT OF
CHRISTIANITY IN UKRAINE BY ST. VOLODYMYR IN
988

Some Famous Street Names

King's Road

Precisely what the name suggests, this was the king's (Charles II) private road or carriage way leading from St James' Palace to Kew and Hampton Court. It did not become a public highway until 1830.

Kensington Gore

A gore is a triangular piece of cloth, and so when Henry III seized a triangular piece of land roughly where the Albert Hall now stands, it was quite logical to call it Kingssegor. In time, this became changed to Kensington Gore.

Gloucester Road

Until the early nineteenth century, this road was called Hogmire Lane. This was a farming district, and in this context 'Hog mire' is a euphemism for pig excrement – hardly the most elegant or desirable association for an up-and-coming part of London! When the Duchess of Gloucester moved to the area, it was felt that this was a good opportunity to suck up to the aristocracy while at the same time giving the whole place a more respectable air, so the road in which she lived was renamed after her Ladyship.

Portobello Road

A farm near here was renamed Porto Bello to commemorate a British victory at a Mexican town of the same name. This was in 1739 and Porto Bello sounded so mellifluous that it was adopted to designate the nearby road as well.

Brompton Road

There was once a tiny hamlet near this road. The lane leading to it was lined with yellow, flowering broom and so the few houses and old alehouse became known as Broom Ton or Broom Town. Brompton is simply a corruption of this.

Knightsbridge

Perhaps the poshest street in RBKC, Knightsbridge is so named because there really was a bridge here. It is claimed that this bridge was called 'knight's bridge' because knights leaving for the crusades crossed it on the way to the Bishop of London's palace at Fulham, where they received a blessing. This may be no more than a neat bit of folk etymology, although it is certainly a picturesque explanation.

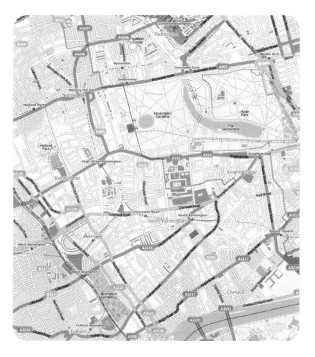

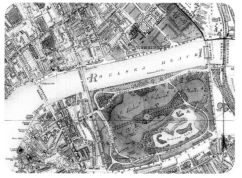

A Hidden River and Two Secret Gardens

Chelsea's Hidden River

Mention of the 'knight's bridge' may well prompt readers to ask themselves, 'bridge over what?' After all, there is no river in this part of London. In fact, a river does flow through the heart of Chelsea, although it has not been seen for many years. The Westbourne rises near Hampstead and flows south from there into the Thames at Chelsea. Although mostly culverted over during the nineteenth century, its route can be traced by street names such as Westbourne Terrace. In 1730, the Westbourne was dammed to create Hyde Park's Serpentine lake and Kensington Long Water. The River Westbourne flows south from Hyde Park, hidden underground for the whole of its route to the Thames – except in one truly astonishing place. It actually passes over the platforms at Sloane Square tube station, carried in an enormous, Victorian iron pipe. The photograph opposite shows this surreal situation: a river flowing over a railway!

Britain's Strangest Garden

A hundred feet or so from High Street Kensington tube station may be found an enchanting garden, possibly the strangest in the entire country. Those in search of this garden will scour the surrounding streets in vain, though, without catching a glimpse of this most unusual place. The reason for this is that it is to be found 100ft *above* the tube station, perched on top of the old Derry & Toms' department store.

Between 1936 and 1938, the owners of Derry & Toms created a roof garden on the top of their Kensington shop. This entailed carrying over 3,000 tons of soil up to the roof in the lifts and planting hundreds of trees and bushes. The result was the largest roof garden in Europe, with three themed gardens, including a Moorish one based on the Alhambra in Spain. A stream was also installed, and flamingos and ducks – with their feathers clipped to stop them flying away – completed the scene. Derry & Toms closed down forty years ago, but the garden is still there. It is open to the public, although the entrance in Derry Street is not very easy to spot. If you wish to visit, it is wise to ring beforehand to check that the gardens are open that day. The telephone number for the Kensington Roof Gardens is 020 7937 7994.

Chelsea Physic Garden

'Physic' being an old synonym for medicine, this garden was originally used for growing herbs for apothecaries. It is the second oldest botanical garden in the country, having been established here in 1673. It contains both the largest fruiting olive tree in Britain, as well as the world's northernmost outdoor grapefruit tree. The tall brick walls surrounding this garden have turned it into a heat trap, allowing exotic plants to flourish here. For the first 300 years of its existence, the Chelsea Physic Garden was completely closed to the public. Since 1983, it has been possible to visit it on some afternoons. It is currently open between 12 and 5 on Tuesday, Wednesday and Friday afternoons from April to October. The entrance is in Swan Walk.

Historical Timeline

First recorded mention
of Kensington found in
the Domesday Book

Queen Mary II
dies of smallpox at
Kensington Palace

Cremorne Gardens open

William III moves
to Kensington

1086 **1689** **1694** **1845**

1661 **1692** **1819** **1849**

Kensington Palace
built; it was
originally called
Nottingham House

Queen Victoria born
in Kensington Palace

Charles Henry Harrod
moves his business to
Brompton Road

First Chelsea
Pensioners admitted
to the recently built
Royal Hospital

28

Royal Horticultural
Society's Spring Show
first held at Chelsea

he world's first
tificial ice-rink
ens in Chelsea

Carpet of flowers
left at Kensington
Palace following
Diana's death

Kensington granted the
title 'Royal Borough'

King's Road is the icon
of the Swinging Sixties

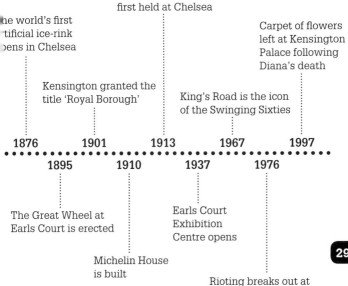

1876   **1901**   **1913**   **1967**   **1997**

          1895   **1910**   **1937**   **1976**

The Great Wheel at
Earls Court is erected

Earls Court
Exhibition
Centre opens

Michelin House
is built

Rioting breaks out at
the Notting Hill Carnival

Demographics

The 12 square kilometres of the Royal Borough of Kensington and Chelsea are home to 158,919 people, 80 per cent of whom are white. According to the 2001 census, just 3 per cent of the population are black Caribbean; this comes as a surprise, considering Notting Hill's connection with Caribbean culture.

Taken overall, the borough has the highest life expectancy in the whole of the UK; however, there are great differences between the various parts of the district. Life expectancy for residents of the affluent area surrounding the Royal Hospital is twelve years greater than that of people in the northernmost part of the borough, where there is a good deal of social housing.

Religious Edifices

RBKC is richly endowed with churches and other places of worship. Among these are:

The Greek Orthodox Cathedral of Saint Sophia
Built in 1882 as simply St Sophia's church, this was declared a cathedral in 1922 and is now the centre of the Greek Orthodox faith in Western Europe. Inside, the cathedral is a typical Greek Orthodox place of worship (with gold leaf, in particular, being used unsparingly).

Brompton Oratory

One of the most impressive Catholic churches in Britain, Brompton Oratory is second only to Westminster Cathedral. It was built in the nineteenth century, in Italian Renaissance style. The ornate, baroque appearance of the church's interior is overwhelming. Brompton oratory is notable for the great width of its nave; it is 51ft wide.

St Mary Abbots

The parish church of Kensington dates from only 1872 and is a splendid example of Victorian Gothic Revival. At 278ft, its spire is the tallest in London. G.K. Chesterton and Ezra Pound both got married here. This was a surprising choice for Pound, who at one time had lived in nearby Kensington Church Walk. He was much irritated by the sound of the bells and once visited the vicar to complain of the 'foul nuisance'. When Princess Diana was killed in a road accident in 1997, St Mary Abbots became a focus for grief, with many people praying here and lighting votive candles. She had been living a short distance away in Kensington Palace.

In addition, RBKC also has many other notable places of worship, including:

A Russian Orthodox church in Knightsbridge

A Spanish and Portuguese synagogue

A Sikh temple

The church – St Lukes – where Charles Dickens was married

The list is extensive.

Even the most obscure and little-known denominations seem to be represented in the borough. Among these are a Moravian church and one dedicated to Estonian Lutherans.

Special mention must be made of the church of the Mormons or Latter Day Saints in Exhibition Road, just across the way from the Science Museum. This place is something of a Mecca for genealogists; it has a huge collection of microfilmed information relating to births and deaths. There is a curious explanation for this: the Mormons believe that it is possible to baptise somebody into the church posthumously, and so devout members of the church track down as many dead family members as possible, in order that they too may be received into the church and thus saved.

The Borough That Never Sleeps

Some London boroughs go to bed at 10 pm with a cup of cocoa and a library book, determined to get a good night's sleep before being up bright and early in the morning. RBKC has never been like that: it is the borough which never sleeps.

The McDonald's opposite High Street Kensington tube station typifies this attitude: it is one of the few McDonald's restaurants which are open twenty-four hours a day. It is special in another way, too: not for Kensington the garish red and yellow frontage which suits lesser parts of London. The Kensington McDonald's was one of the first to be decked out in discrete shades of dark green and gold, which puts one in mind of a bag from Harrods.

24-Hour Timeline

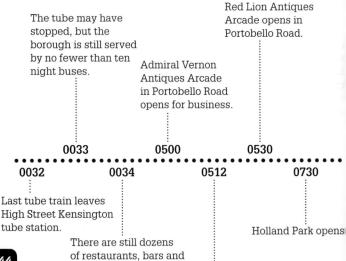

Red Lion Antiques Arcade opens in Portobello Road.

The tube may have stopped, but the borough is still served by no fewer than ten night buses.

Admiral Vernon Antiques Arcade in Portobello Road opens for business.

0033   **0500**   **0530**

0032   **0034**   **0512**   **0730**

Last tube train leaves High Street Kensington tube station.

There are still dozens of restaurants, bars and clubs open in RBKC.

Holland Park opens

First tube trains run in the borough, from Ladbroke Grove.

The museums at South
Kensington open, as
well as the National
Army Museum
in Chelsea and
Kensington Palace.

rtobello Road
arket starts officially,
hough many
rgains will already
ve been snapped up
the early birds.

Harrods food halls close.

0800 **1000** **2100**
• •
0900 **2000** **2300**

Most shops are now
open and the borough
is in full swing.

Many pubs close,
although a lot of
bars and clubs
remain open.

Kensington Central
Library closes.

Who Lives Here?

RBKC has for many years been a very smart place to live. A small book of this sort cannot hope to list all the rich and famous residents of the borough, and so we must content ourselves with a selection.

Tony Benn

Tony Benn's claim to proletarian status has always been a little dubious. During the sixties and seventies he mutated from being the 2nd Viscount Stansgate to plain Anthony Wedgwood Benn. As he moved further to the left, even this was too posh and so he took to calling himself plain Tony Benn. The son of a viscount and grandson of a baronet, he now lives in a £4 million house in Notting Hill. He travels around London by public transport and can often be seen at local bus stops in the area.

P.D. James
The crime writer and member of the House of Lords lives in Kensington.

Michael Winner
A grand Victorian house in Melbury Road is home to the controversial film director. It is decorated in lavish – some might say tasteless – style, and it is rumoured that he plans to leave it on his death to the nation as a museum of his life and career. In 2006, he ungraciously turned down the offer of an OBE, saying, 'An OBE is what you get if you clean the toilets well at King's Cross Station'.

Stella McCartney and Bella Freud
It is perfectly in keeping with the borough's history of trend-setting fashion that two of the youngest and most vibrant of modern fashion designers should live here. Both have homes in Notting Hill.

Two local residents one is unlikely to bump into
Two of Chelsea's most famous residents are also among the most reclusive and secretive. Not surprising, really, since they are both spies.

In the very first *James Bond* book, Ian Fleming, another resident of Chelsea, wrote that Bond lived in, 'a comfortable ground-floor flat in a converted Regency house in a square off the King's Road.' His car was said to be parked nearby, under some plane trees. Careful analysis of this and subsequent texts in the canon has enabled the precise address to be discovered: it is No. 30 Wellington Square.

The address of that other most famous fictional spy, George Smiley from *Tinker, Tailor, Soldier, Spy*, is given explicitly in the text. It is No. 9 Bywater Street, a quiet little cul-de-sac in Chelsea.

TOP SECRET

Street Furniture

One of the many pleasures of walking the streets of RBKC are the minor details to be spotted almost wherever one's eye falls. Take for instance the enormous variety of coal-hole covers to be seen in almost every residential street. At one time, the manufacture of cast-iron covers of this sort was a major industry. A quick glance shows us half a dozen different companies, including a local one, J. Carpenter of Earls Court Road. Presumably, the production of such things now is as surplus to modern requirements as the making of carbon paper and starting handles. A selection of these covers may be seen opposite.

Other unexpected pleasures include one of the oldest pillar boxes in the whole country, an unusual hexagonal one which stands in Kensington High Street and dates from the 1860s. This Victorian survival had a narrow escape during the Blitz of 1940. A German bomb fell nearby and a piece of shrapnel ripped a hole in the base of the pillar box which may be seen to this day.

Two Remarkable Houses

Crosby Hall

It is perhaps no surprise to discover that RBKC boasts the largest private home in the capital. The statistics of this extraordinary building are breathtaking. At its core lies Crosby Hall, a fifteenth-century house which once stood in Bishopsgate, a stone's throw from Liverpool Street station. When it was demolished in the 1920s, it was transported, brick by brick, to Chelsea and re-erected at the end of Cheyne Walk. The building was used by various organisations until it was acquired in 1989 by Christopher Moran, a fabulously wealthy and reclusive businessman. It became his life's work to transform this slightly run down piece of medieval, domestic architecture into a great palace, the grandest home in London.

Nobody knows exactly how much Christopher Moran has spent on creating Crosby Hall. The planning alone took ten years, before work even started. A figure of £25 million has been mentioned, but that is almost certainly a gross underestimate. Every detail of the work had to be painstakingly undertaken using craftsmen trained in medieval and Tudor building techniques. The result so far, for the project is not yet completed, looks as though somebody has plonked an Oxford College down in the heart of London. Crosby Hall has thirty bedrooms and nobody knows how many other rooms. It has been estimated that it would take an hour and a half simply to walk round every room in the place. Christopher Moran has said that he wishes to be buried in the chapel of Crosby Hall when he dies, making it Britain's most expensive and eccentric mausoleum.

CROSBY HALL

PRIVATE PROPERTY

NOT OPEN TO THE PUBLIC

The Tower House

Walking down an unremarkable turning off Kensington High Street, one stumbles across a house which causes many passers-by to stop dead in amazement. Is it a converted church? A copy of a French chateau? It is neither of these things. One of the fathers of the Victorian Gothic Revival movement was architect William Burges. Gothic revival was commonly used on municipal buildings and churches, the idea being to make them look medieval. The Houses of Parliament are a good example of the style: a kind of fantasy castle. Burges believed that Gothic Revival could also be used in domestic architecture and so designed and built Tower House for himself.

The Tower House centres round – as one would guess from the name – a tower. There is a gargoyle, stained glass windows and a spooky interior. It was formerly owned by the actor Richard Harris, who sold it in 1974 to Jimmy Page, guitarist for Led Zeppelin. It is said that David Bowie was also after the house, but was outbid by Page.

Some Other Notable Buildings

There are so many remarkable and unusual buildings in RBKC, and it is hard to know which most deserve a mention. Here are a few truly outstanding examples:

Michelin House

Built in five months in 1910 and opened for business in 1911, the Michelin Building is a triumph of art nouveau design; it was completed on the cusp of the transition to art deco, which style would dominate the coming decades. The external design of Michelin House, the familiar white tiles and stained glass depictions of the famous Michelin Man, must not blind us to the fact that the purpose of this grand building was purely functional. It was a glorified garage, where car owners could have their tyres changed. Michelin House now contains the Conran Shop and Bibendum Restaurant. It may be found at No. 81 Fulham Road.

Earls Court Exhibition Centre

The area of land to the north west of Brompton Cemetery was, for many years, a derelict triangle bounded by railway lines. In the late nineteenth century, a showman called John Robinson Whitley bought it and turned it into a showground. For many years Buffalo Bill's Wild West Show was based here. In 1935, the land changed hands and the new owners decided to continue the tradition of showmanship by building an exhibition centre. It was designed to be the greatest building, by volume, in the whole of Europe.

The art deco building opened in 1937 and has been a popular venue ever since. There are currently plans to demolish it and build high-density housing on the site.

Holland House

Built in 1605, this was once a huge Jacobean Mansion. In the nineteenth century it was a social centre for the upper classes of London, with some of the most exclusive balls and dinner parties in the capital. It was largely destroyed during the Blitz and the parts that remain today can only hint at its former magnificence. Lady Ilchester, who lived at Holland House until her death in 1935, provided P.G. Wodehouse with the model for Bertie Wooster's Aunt Dahlia.

The Royal Court Theatre

The Royal Court Theatre opened on 24 September 1888. In the early years of the twentieth century, many of George Bernard Shaw's plays were produced for the first time at the Royal Court. In 1932, the theatre closed down, and three years later it was converted into a cinema. It was badly damaged by bombing during the Second World War and was practically derelict for the next twelve years.

Four years after it reopened in 1952, the Royal Court saw the first production of *Look back in Anger* by John Osborne. This proved to be seminal work, which gave rise to the expression 'angry young men'.

IN REMEMBRANCE OF 4 5 7
CIVILIANS KILLED IN CHELSEA
BY ENEMY ACTION 1939-1945

In memory of

Anthony Smith, G.C.
who on 23rd February, 1944 carried out an heroic act of rescue
near this building and next to this place and was awarded the
George Cross and the Freedom of the Borough of Chelsea
and

Albert Littlejohn, B.E.M.

The Great Wheel

Although it was demolished over 100 years ago, it is impossible to discuss notable structures in RBKC without mentioning the Great Wheel at Earls Court. Built for the Empire of India exhibition, it was eerily similar to the London Eye. Over 300ft high, it opened to the public in 1895. The forty cars each carried forty passengers, meaning that it could carry 1,600 people at a time; twice as many as the London Eye. It closed down in 1906, after having carried 2.5 million passengers, and was demolished the following year.

The Glaciarium

Another forgotten building, this time at No. 379 King's Road, the Glaciarium was the world's first indoor skating rink with artificially produced ice. It opened in 1876 and soon became a tremendous hit. It was a membership only club, intended to attract wealthy customers who might be familiar with ice skating from holidaying in Switzerland and Austria. It was so successful that John Gamgee, the entrepreneur who started it, soon opened other ice rinks at Charing Cross and also in Manchester. The craze did not last, partly because the cooling method used in the system resulted in thick mists rising from the ice, which at times made the skaters feel that they were moving through a fog. All three rinks closed down in 1878.

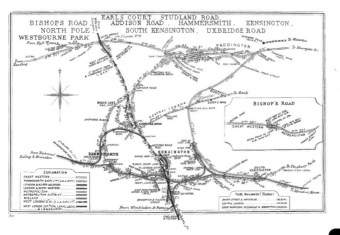

The Pleasure Gardens of Chelsea

The landed gentry have always had space to walk about their estates and enjoy themselves. This was a luxury denied to ordinary people living in the larger European cities of the late eighteenth and early nineteenth centuries. In some such cities, London included, large pleasure gardens were set up as commercial concerns to fulfil the desire to walk under shady trees and participate in the sort of activities in which their betters might indulge. Part funfair, part municipal park and part nightclub, the pleasure gardens of London were, for a while, the favourite diversion of all classes of Londoners.

Two of the most famous of the London pleasure gardens were in Chelsea. Traces of them still remain. **Cremorne Gardens** was on the Chelsea Embankment. It extended from the King's Road all the way to the Thames, where there was a pier for those arriving by boat. Once there, there were restaurants, huge pavilions like miniature versions of the Crystal Palace and, for those with enough pluck, ascents in a hot-air balloon. Cremorne Gardens opened in 1845 and lasted a little over thirty years, closing finally in 1877. It was pressure from the wealthier inhabitants of Chelsea that brought an end to the pleasure gardens. They became increasingly sleazy places, where drunkenness and prostitution became the order of the day. The music and noise from the crowds lasted into the small hours, and towards the end they were a byword for immorality and licentiousness. A tiny fragment of Cremorne Gardens still remains in the form of an award-winning open space by the river, and the original gate has been erected nearby.

Ranelagh Pleasure Gardens were an altogether grander affair. Horace Walpole observed of the place that, 'You can't set your foot without treading on a Prince, or Duke of Cumberland'. The centrepiece of the gardens was the rotunda, a 120ft-wide concert hall where Mozart gave a performance. Ranelagh Gardens survive today as part of the grounds of the Royal Hospital; the Chelsea Flower Show has been held here since 1913.

ELEPHANT & CASTLE

MANOR STREET, OLD KENT ROAD.

NOVEL & SCIENTIFIC EXHIBITION.

The Splendid Model of the

PARACHUTE

OR

FLYING MACHINE.

With which the late Mons. Le. TUR, ascended from

CREMORNE GARDENS

On the 27th June last, will be exhibited in the large Room, of the above House on MONDAY Next, the 28th AUGUST, 1854, and during the Week.

The MODEL made by Mr. ADAMS, the Æronaut (who so successfully took up Mons. LE TUR, on the first occasion), is made upon a scale of 1 inch to the Foot, and is 7 feet high.

Green Spaces

RBKC has two large cemeteries and a 55-acre park. In addition to this, there are the grounds of the Royal Hospital, including Ranelagh Gardens, and also the Kensington Palace and its gardens. For such a small borough, there are an incredible number of gardens to be found hidden in little squares and tucked away down side streets. Almost without exception, these are private and reserved for the use of nearby residents. Walking the streets of Kensington and Chelsea can accordingly be a tantalising and frustrating experience. One stumbles constantly across delightful little gardens at which one can only peek hopelessly, with no hope of being able to get in. It makes one feel a little like Alice when she peered through the tiny door into a beautiful garden which she could never enter.

The centre of London is a 'heat island', consistently a couple of degrees warmer than the rest of south-east England. This means that plants and trees flourish here which are not commonly seen elsewhere in the country. This effect is accentuated by the brick walls surrounding gardens, which tend to retain the heat. Fruiting olive trees are to be found in front gardens, and vines yielding huge bunches of grapes. In Holland Park are towering banana plants, while the Chelsea Physic Garden has the world's most northerly outdoor grapefruit tree.

Perhaps it is the effect of the Chelsea Flower Show being held in the borough each year, but residents seem to compete with each other to see how flowery and verdant they are able to make their gardens, houses, commercial premises and even tube stations. The platform at South Kensington station, for instance, resembles a country halt, with masses of blooms and shrubs. Halfway down Kensington Church Street is the Churchill Arms, a pub which is literally covered in flowers.

The most northerly green space in the borough is Kensal Green Cemetery, which is both a haven for wildlife and also crammed with famous dead residents.

Jean-Francois Gravelet is here. He is better known as Blondin, the daredevil who crossed the Niagara Falls many times on a tightrope. Today, he rubs shoulders with **Wilkie Collins**, author of *The Moonstone* and *The Woman in White*. Those most famous of Victorian engineers have come to rest here: **Marc Isambard Brunel** and his son, **Isambard Kingdom Brunel**. Both once lived in Chelsea. **Anthony Trollope** is here, and so is **William Makepeace Thackeray**, another long-time resident of the borough.

At the other end of RBKC is Brompton Cemetery, which is now managed by the Royal Parks and is more of a park these days than a graveyard.

Beatrix Potter, who lived nearby, used names from the gravestones here for characters in her stories. Headstones here include the names of Mr Nutkins, Jeremiah Fisher, Mr McGregor and Peter Rabbet.

Wildlife

For such a small, inner-city district, Kensington and Chelsea have quite a lot of unusual animals and birds. This is perhaps because of the chain of cemeteries, parks and squares which span the borough. Tawny owls and woodpeckers are found in Holland Park, as well as sparrowhawks and peacocks. A survey in 1997 discovered that weasels were living in Kensal Green Cemetery, the closest that they have been found to the centre of London. An unusual population of feral rabbits have colonised Holland Park. They are clearly the descendents of domesticated rabbits, as blacks and whites predominate. How they escape the attentions of the ubiquitous urban foxes in this part of London is something of a mystery.

The most exotic creatures to be found in the borough are flamingos and parrots. Holland Park and Kensington Palace gardens are both home to flocks of rose-ringed parakeets, a type of parrot. Nobody knows where these birds, now common throughout London and the Home Counties, originated. One theory is that when the film *The African Queen* was being made at Shepperton studios in 1951, twenty parakeets, which were being used to add verisimilitude to a shot, escaped and started breeding.

Flocks of parrots in the park are nothing compared to the colony of Chilean flamingos that have made their home on the roof of the old Derry & Toms' department store in Kensington High Street. They were introduced when the roof garden opened before the war, and there have been flamingos there ever since.

Popular Events

The royal borough plays host to two events which each year attract national – and sometimes worldwide – attention.

These are the **Chelsea Flower Show** and the **Notting Hill Carnival**. Chelsea also continues to celebrate a national holiday which was formally abolished in the rest of the country in 1859. This is Oak-Apple Day or Royal Oak Day, of which, more later.

The Chelsea Flower Show

The Royal Horticultural Society Chelsea Flower Show is held over a period of five days every May. It was once known as the Great Spring Show and has only been held at Chelsea since 1913. It was cancelled in 1917 and 1918, the closing years of the First World War, and during the Second World War it was not held at all, due to the fact that the land was being used as an anti-aircraft gun emplacement. There was some doubt after the war as to whether the event would be held again, but in 1947 the Chelsea Flower Show was held and proved a great success – the perfect antidote to postwar austerity.

The Notting Hill Carnival

After the Notting Hill 'race riots' in 1958, some members of the West Indian community in North Kensington decided to celebrate their identity more overtly, rather than simply try and blend in by behaving exactly like the British. In 1959, a Mardi Gras festival was held, and over the next few years this developed into the carnival which we know today. It takes place over the August Bank Holiday and is traditionally a time for everybody to get together and enjoy themselves. From 1976 onwards, however, it has periodically been marred by violence – both against the police and also against ordinary carnival-goers. Outbreaks of mugging and occasional stabbings have made many a little dubious as to its value for enhancing community cohesion.

Oak-Apple Day

The Royal Hospital, home to 400 Chelsea Pensioners, was founded by King Charles II in 1682. Following the restoration of Charles to the throne in 1660, parliament declared the King's birthday, on 29 May, to be a public holiday. It was celebrated with oak leaves and oak apples (which are a kind of gall), in memory of his escape from Roundhead forces after the Battle of Worcester by hiding in an oak tree. For two centuries, this festival was kept in Britain, before being abolished by the Victorians. It lingers on in Chelsea as Founder's Day. The Chelsea Pensioners parade and are then inspected by a member of the royal family. In 2010, this was undertaken by Prince Harry – the first time in many years that a serving officer has performed the duty. All those taking part wear sprigs of oak leaves.

Opera in the Park

For some years, Holland Park has been host to open-air opera productions in the summer. It is a kind of small-scale version of Glyndebourne. Holland House itself provides a dramatic backdrop, used to particular effect in operas such as Donizetti's *Roberto Devereaux*, which is set in the early seventeenth century and roughly contemporaneous with the house itself.

Literary Links and Artistic Associations

So many writers and artists have lived in RBKC that it would probably be easier to list those who have not at some time lived in the borough, rather than put down all those who have. Here are some of the more famous authors and artists who were born, lived, worked, married or died in Kensington and Chelsea:

Charles Dickens was married at St Luke's church, Sydney Street, in 1836.

William Makepeace Thackeray, author of *Vanity Fair*, lived in Onslow Square for nine years, from 1853-1862.

George Orwell, who coined phrases such as 'Big Brother' and 'thought crime', lived for a while in Portobello Road.

Elizabeth Gaskell, creator of *Cranford*, had a house in Cheyne Walk.

George Eliot, who wrote *Mill on the Floss*, lived and died at Cheyne Walk.

Henry James, known for *The Turn of the Screw*, lived in RBKC.

G.K. Chesterton was both born in Kensington and also lived and wrote there. His most famous book, *The Napoleon of Notting Hill*, is set entirely in the borough.

Saint Thomas More,
Chancellor of England
martyred for his Faith on
Tower Hill 1535, lived here.
It was from his house here
that he went for his trial
and his imprisonment in the
Tower of London.

Bram Stoker, remembered chiefly for *Dracula*, lived at Cheyne Walk in Chelsea.

James Joyce lived in Campden Grove, which he found so dull that he renamed it Campden Grave.

Thomas More, author of the classic *Utopia*, had a house near Cheyne Walk in the sixteenth century.

Oscar Wilde lived in Tite Street and was arrested at the Cadogan Hotel after the collapse of his libel action against the Marquess of Queensberry.

Many famous poets have lived in the borough, including **Robert Browning**, **T.S. Eliot**, **Ezra Pound**, **John Betjeman**, **Hilaire Belloc**, **Algernon Swinburne** and **Dylan Thomas**. The area has also attracted humorists and authors of children's books. **P.G. Wodehouse** lived here, and so did **Mark Twain**. The writers of *Winnie the Pooh*, *The Wind in the Willows* and *The Water Babies* all had homes in RBKC, and **Beatrix Potter** lived the first thirty-nine years of her life in Earls Court.

Among other well-known writers who have spent time in the borough are **Ian Fleming**, **Agatha Christie**, **Laurie Lee**, **Harold Pinter** and **Siegfried Sassoon**.

Some Very Odd Pets and a Children's Story

Following the death of his wife in 1862, **Dante Gabriel Rossetti**, the famous pre-Raphaelite artist, turned his home at No. 16 Cheyne Walk, Chelsea, into a miniature zoo. He kept parakeets, deer and jackasses in the back garden, and allowed an armadillo and two wombats the run of the house.

Sir John Tenniel, the artist who illustrated *Alice in Wonderland*, was a visitor to the house, as was **Lewis Carroll**. It is rumoured that Tenniel used one of the wombats as the model for the dormouse at the Mad Hatter's tea party.

The Private Life of *Dracula*'s Creator

Like so many other famous writers, Bram Stoker used to live in Cheyne Walk, at No. 27. He helped to rescue a drowning man from the Thames one day, which runs only a few yards from Cheyne Walk. He carried the man into his house and laid him on the dining table to recover. He then left the room. However, far from recovering, the man died. Mrs Stoker then entered the dining room without knowing any of this, and discovered a corpse lying on her table. The family moved out a short while later.

Artists in Chelsea

Since the mid-nineteenth century, Chelsea has had a bohemian reputation. All three founding members of the Pre-Raphaelite Brotherhood – **John Millais**, **Dante Gabrielle Rossetti** and **William Holman Hunt** – lived and worked in RBKC. The Brotherhood centred for a time around Rossetti's house in Cheyne Walk. **Turner**, **James McNeill Whistler** and **Frederic, Lord Leighton**, all lived nearby at different times.

Books, Plays and Films

The Napoleon of Notting Hill

Perhaps the most famous book written and set in RBKC is *The Napoleon of Notting Hill* by G.K. Chesterton, best known for his *Father Brown* stories and born in Kensington, where he also lived and married. In this fantasy, London is divided into small chiefdoms whose leaders war upon each other.

Passing Brompton Road

There was once a tube station in Brompton Road, between Knightsbridge and South Kensington. It was so little used that many trains did not bother to stop there. Staff would cry, 'Passing Brompton Road' to warn passengers who wished to get off at this stop. This became something of a catchphrase among Londoners, and *Passing Brompton Road* was the title of a successful farce in the 1920s.

Made in Chelsea

Made in Chelsea is a reality documentary TV series about a group of young people living in Chelsea.

The L-Shaped Room

A novel by Lynne Reid Banks which is set almost entirely in Notting Hill.

Notting Hill

A 1999 film shot almost entirely in RBKC; many of the scenes are filmed in Portobello Road. The outside shots of the protagonist's home are of director Richard Curtis' house at No. 280 Westbourne Park Road.

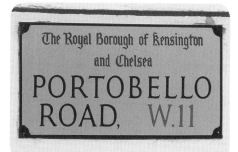

The Royal Borough of Kensington and Chelsea

PORTOBELLO ROAD, W.11

Museums and Galleries

RBKC is, of course, home to so-called museum land: the 150-year-old complex of museums at South Kensington.

These include the **Natural History Museum**, now combined with the old **Geological Museum**, the **Science Museum** and the **Victoria and Albert**.

Less well-known is the **National Army Museum** in Chelsea. Chelsea has a strong military history and was the logical place for such a museum. **Kensington Palace** too is partly a museum, although various minor members of the royal family also live there.

The borough contains two unusual museums, both in the former homes of eminent Victorians. One of these is **Thomas Carlyle's House** at No. 24 Cheyne walk. Carlyle, perhaps the most famous Victorian Man of Letters of all, moved into the Queen Anne house in 1834 and lived there with his family for the next thirty-seven years. After his death it was acquired for the nation and preserved precisely as it had been at Carlyle's death.

Leighton House, the former home of the Victorian artist Frederick, Lord Leighton, has also been preserved for posterity. The house, which Leighton had specially built, is unique. The most famous feature is undoubtedly the Arab Hall. Leighton brought back hundreds of decorative tiles from his travels in Syria and these have all been set into the walls of the Arab Hall. The effect is dazzlingly exotic. The house is also an art gallery.

Near Sloane Square in Chelsea is a unique art gallery, the only free gallery of contemporary art of this size in the world. It is the **Saatchi Gallery**, and it occupies fifteen large rooms in the former Duke of York's HQ. The philosophy of the gallery is simple: to show modern art which would not be seen in other London galleries such as the **Tate Modern**. The aim is to make cutting-edge art accessible to all.

It is impossible to write of the museums and galleries of RBKC without mentioning one which is now closed. From 1893, the **Imperial Institute** was to be found in Exhibition Road, next to the other South Kensington museums. With the end of the Empire following the Second World War, the Institute's name was changed to the **Commonwealth Institute**, which (from 1962) occupied a distinctive building on the edge of Holland Park. This museum contained exhibits from every nation of the British Commonwealth and was hugely popular. Extensive building work and renovations were carried out on the building in 2001, following which it simply closed for good under circumstances which have never really been explained.

Blue Plaques

Cheyne Walk in Chelsea is reputed to have more blue plaques than any other street in Britain.

Whether or not this is so, RBKC is certainly littered with the things. Blue plaques, of course, mark the locations in London where famous people were born, lived, worked or died. It is impossible to walk along most streets in the borough without noticing one or two of them. Most of the blue plaques draw attention to people who are more or less household names. Cheyne Walk, mentioned above, boasts, for example, plaques to such well-known individuals as engineer **Marc Brunel** and his son **Isambard Kingdom Brunel**, **Hilaire Belloc**, and artists **Dante Gabrielle Rossetti**, **Turner** and **Whistler**, who were also former residents of the street.

Some of those whose lives have been immortalised in this way are perhaps a little less memorable. Even Cheyne Walk has some notably forgettable figures among its blue plaques: sculptor **John Tweed** (1863-1933), for instance, or artist **Philip Wilson Steer** (1860-1942).

The picture is much the same elsewhere in the borough, with the world famous rubbing shoulders with the frankly unknown. Who now remembers the achievements, or indeed even the name, of **Colonel R.E.B. Crompton** (1845-1940), an electrical engineer who once lived in Kensington Court? What shall we say of **John Simon** (1816-1904), a pioneer of public health who once lived in Kensington Square?

Some of the juxtapositions of blue plaques in Kensington and Chelsea are jaw-droppingly bizarre. On the side of an unremarkable block of Victorian flats in Melbury Road, just off Kensington High Street, are two blue plaques, one above the other. One tells us that **William Holman Hunt**, a founder of the Pre-Raphaelite artistic movement, lived here during the late nineteenth century. This is all very right and proper; the pre-Raphaelites mostly lived in RBKC at one time or another. The other plaque though tells us that while Holman Hunt was living here in 1882, **King Cetshwayo**, leader of the Zulu nation, moved in next door. One cannot help but wonder at this peculiar circumstance. Did the exiled king of the Zulus pop round to Holman Hunt's studio in order to borrow a cup of sugar or a shilling for the gas meter?

Famous for...

Chelsea FC

Oscar Wilde

The Notting Hill Carnival

Chelsea Pensioners

Sloane Rangers

Floral tributes at the death of Princess Diana

Museums

Harrods

The Pre-Raphaelites

Writers

Earls Court Exhibition Centre

The King's Road

Portobello Road Market

Infamous for...

The Cadogan Hotel

Opened as an upmarket place to stay in 1887, the hotel in Sloane Street became notorious eight years later. Oscar Wilde had brought an action for libel against the Marquess of Queensbury for describing him – accurately – as 'a sodomite'. The case collapsed as it became obvious that Wilde was in the habit of amusing himself with male prostitutes. After the failure of his action, it was clearly only a matter of time before Oscar Wilde was arrested for what was, at that time, a serious offence. His friends urged him to flee the country; instead he sat drinking in room 118 of the Cadogan Hotel. He was arrested there by two Scotland Yard detectives on 6 April 1895. The charge was gross indecency, for which he was later sent to prison for two years. The arrest itself was immortalised in a poem by John Betjeman.

The Cadogan Hotel was also home to Lillie Langtry, who lived there from 1892 to 1897. Although nominally an actress, Langtry's real talent lay in ensnaring wealthy and aristocratic lovers. These included the Prince of Wales, later Edward VII. Other lovers were the Earl of Shrewsbury and Prince Lois of Battenberg. Combined with Wilde's arrest, the effect was to give the Cadogan Hotel a rather *demi-monde* reputation.

LILLIE LANGTRY

1852

Notting Hill Riots

The first riots to take place in Britain after the Second World War were in Notting Hill. These so-called 'race riots' took place in the summer of 1958 and were a consequence of the aggressive reactions of some young hooligans to the sudden influx of West Indian immigrants in the 1950s. Empty bottles were thrown, and several young men were stabbed. Nine young white men received sentences of five years' imprisonment apiece, which had the effect of discouraging violence of this sort.

Eighteen years later, the first real riot to occur in Britain for over fifty years exploded in Notting Hill. It began during the carnival in 1976. Police had attempted to arrest a young black pickpocket, who was rescued by his friends. This trivial incident was the signal for widespread attacks on the police, which left over sixty needing hospital treatment. Police vehicles were overturned and set on fire, a thing never before seen on the British mainland. No riot shields or other equipment were available, and so the police were forced to improvise shields by using milk crates and dustbin lids. There was an outbreak of window smashing and theft during the disturbances. This was the first serious riot of the twentieth century to take place in England.

Punks

King's Road had two bites at the cherry as far as being an iconic centre for fashion is concerned. In 1967, it became, along with Carnaby Street in Soho, the epitome of the Swinging Sixties. Then, ten years later, it once again hit the headlines for a new style of fashion: that of the so-called 'punks'. The garish and outrageous clothing and bizarre hairstyles of these young people were seen as an affront to the staid and middle-aged. Nowhere were they more in evidence than on the King's Road.

In 1971, Vivienne Westwood and Malcolm McClaren opened a boutique on King's Road called Let it Rock. They later changed the name to SEX. McClaren went on to manage the Sex Pistols and the boutique became the very epicentre of punk culture. Even today, almost forty years later, a best-selling London postcard shows two punks in King's Road with brightly dyed hair. This image has become a shorthand symbol for young and outrageous London.

A Question of Sport

Chelsea FC

Mention of Chelsea for many people means just one thing: the football team of that name, Chelsea FC. Based at Stamford Bridge stadium in Fulham, Chelsea are one of the country's top teams. Winners of the FA Cup six times, four times English champions and twice winners of the UEFA Cup, Chelsea FC are certainly a force to be reckoned with in English football.

However, it was not always so: before the war, Chelsea FC were a byword for failure, and a comic song was released by Norman Long entitled 'The Day that Chelsea Went and Won the Cup'. Various bizarre and improbable events were described, culminating in Chelsea winning the FA Cup.

One of the first films about football ever made, *The Great Game* (1930), was set at Stamford Bridge and featured several Chelsea players.

The 2012 Olympics

The Olympic Road Cycling Race will pass through RBKC during the opening days of the Olympic Games. The route will enter the borough at Knightsbridge, pass along Brompton Road and then head west into Fulham. Volleyball will be played at the Earls Court Exhibition Centre. Plans are afoot to demolish this landmark building after the Olympics, and so the volleyball matches played there might well be by way of a swansong for Earls Court.

Military matters

Chelsea has had strong military connections for some centuries. In 1682, Charles II founded the Royal Hospital as a kind of almshouse for old soldiers. Legend has it that this was done at the instigation of the king's mistress, Nell Gwynne. Christopher Wren designed the building, in which 400 veterans still live. Their distinctive red coats and tricorn hats are based upon early eighteenth-century military uniforms.

There were two large barracks in the Chelsea: the Duke of York's Barracks and the Chelsea Barracks. The Duke of York's Barracks was at one time used as an orphanage for the children of soldiers. In 1945, one of the last capital trials for treachery was held here, when Theodore Schurch was court-martialled. He was found guilty and subsequently hanged. Part of the old barracks is now used by the Saatchi Gallery.

Until very recently, the Chelsea Barracks were a distinctive landmark in the area. They too have been sold off to property developers and luxury flats are being erected on the site. Only the National Army Museum now remains to remind people of the military associations of this part of London.

Dear Sir...

The inhabitants of the Royal Borough of Kensington
and Chelsea may in general be very affluent, influential
and important, but – judging by their letters to the local
newspapers – their interests are every bit as parochial as the
residents of any other London borough. A look back at the
letters page of the *Kensington and Chelsea Chronicle* over
the last year or so gives a good flavour of their concerns.

On 3 March 2011, for example, one resident from Delgarno
Gardens expressed his irritation at the children hanging
round the streets during February's half-term holiday. We
are given to understand that when he was a child there were
no such things as half-term holidays. No wonder children
these days are hopeless at English; they are never in school!

A couple of days later the same resident wrote again, this
time about noisy neighbours in Delgarno Gardens. Then, on
12 March, he took up his pen to compose another letter about
dogs fouling the pavement; can nothing be done about this
nuisance? There seems to be no aspect of life in the Royal
Borough about which this writer is not ready to complain.

A quick glance at the last year or so's letters to the local
press reveals similar kinds of complaints: air pollution in
Earls Court, a new railway station at Kensal Green and
traffic congestion on Cromwell Road. It is reassuring to
observe that the lives and concerns of residents noted for
their wealth and longevity should be every bit as trifling and
inconsequential as those of us who live in less salubrious
parts of the United Kingdom!

Headline News

Arrest of Mr Oscar Wilde: *The Times*, 6 April 1895

The piece below goes on to give details of Wilde's arrest at the Cadogan Hotel in Sloane Street. It continues with the ominous news that, 'Mr Oscar Wilde's name was yesterday removed from the play-bills and programmes of the Haymarket and St James's Theatres. And this before even being tried; let alone found guilty!'

Why the Chelsea Flower Show matters: *The Times*, 16 May 2009

One of many articles in praise of the Chelsea Flower Show:

'I start getting excited about Chelsea from the moment I buy my ticket in the depths of winter…the nation joins me in my gardening obsession… there is no more splendid sight than the Great Pavilion… Love it or hate it, the show gets people talking about gardens — and that's my favourite topic…'

'Backstreet Hamlet Talks Bosh'

Headline of one of the first reviews of what was to become a defining cultural event of the 1950s: the opening night of John Osborne's *Look Back in Anger*.

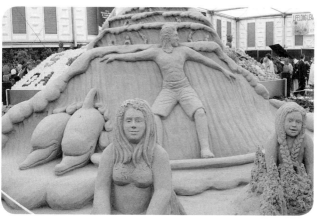

Assorted Kensington and Chelsea-Related Trivia

Chelsea tractors are large, ostentatious 4x4 vehicles which are used in urban areas rather than off-road. They are frequently seen on school runs in wealthier parts of London.

Kensington was a board game devised in 1979. It enjoyed quite a vogue, before being all but forgotten. A game of strategy, it had similarities with the ancient game of Nine Men's Morris.

Chelsea Buns were first made at the Chelsea Bun House in the eighteenth century. They are rich and spicy and were much favoured by aristocrats – and even royalty – when Chelsea was still a village.

Kensington Gore was once a trademark name for a type of theatrical blood devised by a chemist called John Tyngate. It was popular in horror films during the sixties and seventies. Since Tyngate's death, the term has become a generic name for fake blood.

Chelsea Porcelain was the first porcelain manufactured in this country. A factory was set up in Chelsea for this purpose in 1743, and for the next forty years it produced fine porcelain figures similar to those from Sévres. The business then relocated to Derby in the north of England.

Kensington Quartets is what T.S. Eliot originally planned to call the four linked poems which became known as the *Four Quartets*. Eliot lived in Kensington for many years, eventually dying at No. 37 Kensington Court Place.

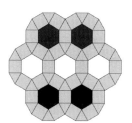

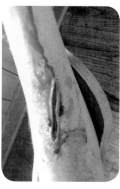

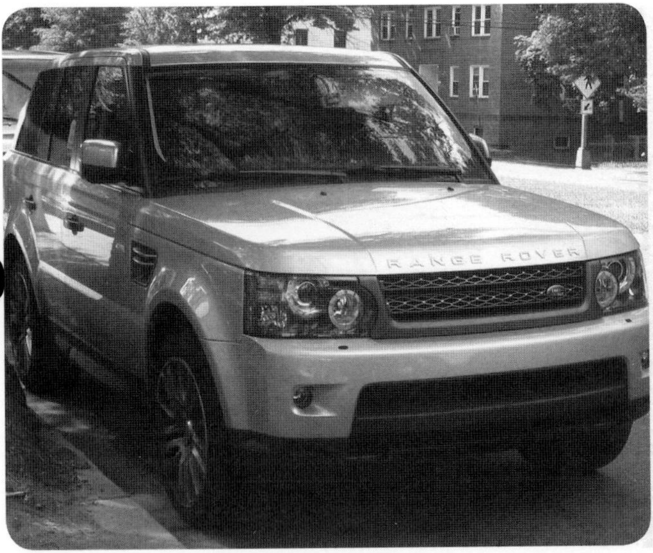
RANGE ROVER

Image Captions and Credits